National Parks
Martin Luther King, Jr. Memorial

CHRISTINE TAYLOR-BUTLER

Children's Press®
An Imprint of Scholastic Inc.

Content Consultant

James Gramann, PhD

Professor Emeritus, Department of Recreation, Park and Tourism Sciences

Texas A&M University, College Station, Texas

Library of Congress Cataloging-in-Publication Data

Names: Taylor-Butler, Christine, author.

Title: Martin Luther King, Jr. Memorial / by Christine Taylor-Butler.

Description: New York, NY : Children's Press, an imprint of Scholastic Inc., [2019] | Series: A true book | Includes index.

Identifiers: LCCN 2018032563| ISBN 9780531129340 (library binding) | ISBN 9780531135037 (pbk.)

Subjects: LCSH: Martin Luther King, Jr., Memorial (Washington, D.C.)—Juvenile literature. | Memorials—Washington (D.C.)—Juvenile literature.

Classification: LCC F203.4.M118 T38 2019 | DDC 975.3—dc23

LC record available at https://lccn.loc.gov/2018032563

All rights reserved. Published in 2019 by Children's Press, an imprint of Scholastic Inc.

Printed in Heshan, China 62

SCHOLASTIC, CHILDREN'S PRESS, A TRUE BOOK™, and associated logos are trademarks and/or registered trademarks of Scholastic Inc.

Scholastic Inc., 557 Broadway, New York, NY 10012

1 2 3 4 5 6 7 8 9 10 R 28 27 26 25 24 23 22 21 20 19

Front cover (main): Statue at the Martin Luther King, Jr. Memorial

Front cover (inset): Martin Luther King Jr. speaking at the March on Washington

Back cover: A badge in support of Martin Luther King Jr.

Find the Truth!

Everything you are about to read is true *except* for one of the sentences on this page.

Which one is **TRUE**?

T or F The Martin Luther King, Jr. Memorial was made in China.

T or F The monument was approved and built just 10 years after King's death.

Find the answers in this book.

3

Contents

THE BIG TRUTH!

Washington Monument

The monument's sculptor (left) and chief architect

The completed statue

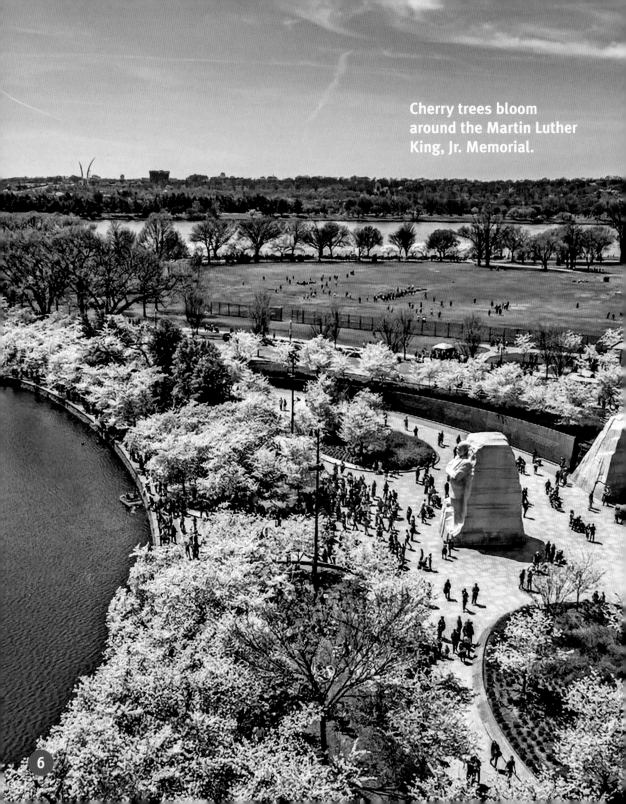

Cherry trees bloom around the Martin Luther King, Jr. Memorial.

CHAPTER 1

A Leader for Civil Rights

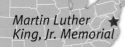

Martin Luther King, Jr. Memorial

Towering over onlookers near the Potomac River in Washington, D.C., is the Martin Luther King, Jr. Memorial. It is located at 1964 Independence Avenue SW. The address is important. In 1964, the U.S. government passed the **Civil Rights** Act. This ended **segregation** and other forms of unfair treatment. Today, the **monument** honors a man who fought for the equality not only of fellow African Americans, but of all people.

Martin Jr. (front row, right) poses for a photo with his siblings, parents, and grandmother (back row, right).

Becoming Dr. King

Martin Luther King Jr. was born Michael King Jr. in 1929 in Atlanta, Georgia. He and his father both changed their names to Martin Luther King when Michael Jr. was little. Young Martin grew up listening to his father preach against segregation. Many years later, after becoming a minister himself, Dr. King preached that peaceful protests were a good way to fight for equal rights.

At first, however, King did not plan to be a minister. A gifted student, he entered Morehouse College in Atlanta at the age of 15. There, he studied sociology, the study of society and culture. Dr. Benjamin Mays, president of the college, asked Morehouse students to pay attention to society's problems. He told them it was their job to correct the sufferings and injustices they found.

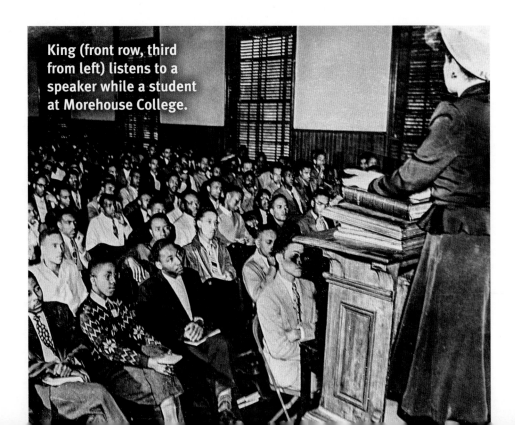

King (front row, third from left) listens to a speaker while a student at Morehouse College.

Dr. Mays introduced King to the teachings of Indian **activist** Mahatma Gandhi. Gandhi believed in the power of nonviolent protest. Dr. Mays's influence led King to study religion in graduate school. He went to Crozer Theological Seminary in Pennsylvania and then Boston University in Massachusetts. Living in these northern states gave King a sense of freedom he did not feel in Georgia. While working on his doctorate, King decided to become a civil rights activist.

Mahatma Gandhi (with walking stick) walks along Juhu Beach in Mumbai, India.

Fighting for Equality

Over the next decade, King worked with other civil rights leaders to end racial **discrimination**. He helped organizers in Birmingham, Alabama, end segregation on buses with a **boycott**. He helped create the

King wrote about equal rights even while in jail.

Southern Christian Leadership Conference, a civil rights organization. He protested police violence, fought for fair hiring practices, and organized protests against the war in Vietnam. For his efforts, he was thrown in jail. Still, he continued speaking out.

King delivers his "I Have a Dream" speech.

On the steps of the Lincoln Memorial is a marker that shows where King stood to give his "I Have a Dream" speech.

I Have a Dream

In 1963, organizers for a protest in Washington, D.C., selected Dr. King as their main speaker. The protest was called the March on Washington for Jobs and Freedom. King delivered his speech, "I Have a Dream," on the steps of the Lincoln Memorial. More than 250,000 people were present. King's work and words caught the attention of the Nobel Committee in Norway. In 1964, the committee awarded him the Nobel Peace Prize. At the time, he was the youngest person ever to receive it.

A Life Cut Short

Although Dr. King preached nonviolence, some people felt threatened by his message. In 1968, King traveled to Memphis, Tennessee. He hoped to help sanitation workers, who keep streets and water clean, fight for decent wages and other rights. On April 4, King went out onto the balcony of the Lorraine Hotel, where he was staying. He was shot and killed there. Decades after his death, King's message of racial equality continues to inspire millions of people.

People point in the direction of the sound of a gunshot after King is assassinated.

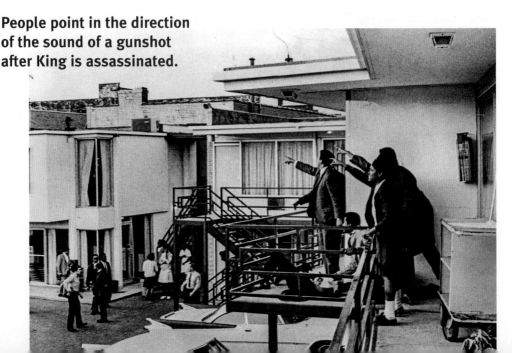

It was not until 2000 that all 50 states recognized King's birthday as a holiday.

CHAPTER 2

Honoring the Past and Future

In the years after Dr. King's death, many people wanted to build a memorial for him. But this wasn't easy. It took almost 30 years of planning. In 1983, interest in a memorial spiked when the U.S. Congress passed a law making King's birthday a national holiday. That year, members of the Alpha Phi Alpha **fraternity** sat around a dining room table and made plans for a memorial. King had joined the fraternity in 1952 while attending Boston University.

Efforts Continue

It was more than 10 years later before Congress passed a **resolution** allowing the government to provide land for the memorial. This was a major victory for memorial planners. But Congress took even longer to approve fund-raising and selecting a location to build. They gave King's old fraternity until November 2003 to raise $100 million. The fraternity created a special foundation for this task. The organization reached its goal—and beyond, raising $120 million.

Members of the Alpha Phi Alpha fraternity stand onstage during a celebration for the memorial.

Lincoln Memorial

Site for King's memorial

Tidal Basin

Jefferson Memorial

Potomac River

The Lincoln, King, and Jefferson memorials more or less form a straight line.

In 1999, land in the National Mall was approved for the memorial. The National Mall is an area of parkland and monuments in Washington, D.C. King's monument would be on the shore of the Tidal Basin, near the Potomac River. From there, visitors can see the Thomas Jefferson and Abraham Lincoln memorials. This location connects three moments in history: Jefferson declaring all men are equal in 1776, Lincoln freeing the slaves in the 1860s, and King fighting for equality.

An international panel soon formed to coordinate the work. More than 900 artists from 52 countries submitted designs. Panel members selected entry #1403. This design was created by ROMA Design Group in California. A government committee reviewed the design, approving it six years later in 2006. The design needed an artist to do the sculpting. So in 2007, planners chose Chinese artist Lei Yixin to be the memorial's sculptor.

A small model shows what designers had in mind for the monument.

A Master Sculptor

Lei Yixin was born in Changsha, China, in 1954. He worked on a farm but spent his free time drawing in a scrapbook. In 1978, those drawings helped him gain acceptance into art school in China. After winning many awards, the Chinese government selected him as a master sculptor, an important position. Before he carved the Martin Luther King, Jr. Memorial, Lei sculpted more than 150 monuments for his country.

Lei's signature in the memorial's stone

Scaffolding surrounded the statue of King as construction workers put the monument together in Washington, D.C.

King is buried in Atlanta, Georgia, near his boyhood home, which is now a national historical park.

CHAPTER 3

One Hundred Fifty-Nine Blocks of Granite

The selection of a Chinese artist made some people angry. They complained that an African American sculptor should have been chosen to create Dr. King's memorial. The committee reminded everyone that King's dream was for people to be judged on their character, not the color of their skin. Lei Yixin had experience carving large granite sculptures. Other artists had recommended him. Lei was finally approved as the memorial's lead sculptor.

Lei stands next to a 3-foot (1 m) model of his statue of Martin Luther King.

Studying the Subject

Lei studied King's writings and photographs. Then he created 3-foot (1 meter) and 30-foot (9 m) **models** of his planned statue. He sent these to the U.S. Commission of Fine Arts, which had to approve every monument in Washington, D.C. Some commission members thought Lei made King look too bullying. Others thought King didn't look powerful enough. But Ed Jackson, the chief architect, explained that the image came from a photo of King. This convinced the commission to approve the statue.

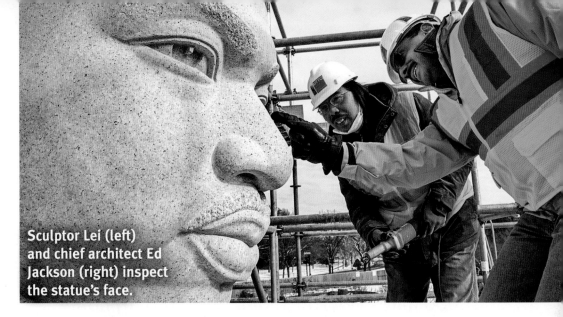

Sculptor Lei (left) and chief architect Ed Jackson (right) inspect the statue's face.

 The granite used for Dr. King's head weighed 46 tons.

Shaping Stone

Exactly 159 blocks of Chinese granite were shipped to Lei's studio in China. Lei hired 10 Chinese sculptors to work with him. Many were university professors. Lei and the other artists carved King's sculpture out of a dark shrimp-pink granite called G-681. This helped showcase King's African American features. The other sculptors worked on the body of the memorial. Only Lei worked on the face.

Each piece of the sculpture has a concrete core with a layer of granite over it. This made the pieces lighter in weight. Solid granite would have been too heavy to ship to the United States. When the sculpture was 80 percent finished, it was taken apart. These parts were shipped roughly 11,000 miles (17,703 kilometers) to Baltimore, Maryland, for reassembly. It took the crews there close to six weeks to assemble the stones.

Stones were packed in crates for the long journey from China to the United States.

Lei and Jackson stand next to the completed statue (right). The statue was based on a photo of King (above).

Error!

After the statue was assembled, the planning committee spotted a mistake. The photo that architects had sent Lei showed King holding a pen in his left hand. But King was right-handed. He would have held the pen in his right hand. The photo had been reversed, making everything backward. It was too late to change the pen to the right hand. Lei solved the issue by turning the pen into a scroll of paper.

Set in Stone

Nick Benson, a Rhode Island stone carver, spent two years engraving King's quotes into the memorial's statue and the wall behind it. One quote on the statue read, "I was a drum major for justice, peace and righteousness." The original quote had been much longer. Lei had requested the quote be shortened so it would fit better.

Nick Benson has worked on multiple memorials in the National Mall.

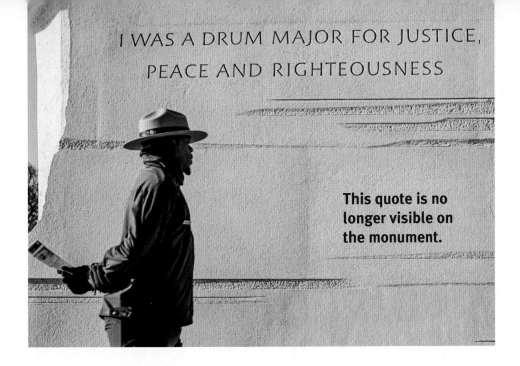

I WAS A DRUM MAJOR FOR JUSTICE, PEACE AND RIGHTEOUSNESS

This quote is no longer visible on the monument.

When the statue was unveiled in 2011, some people demanded the "drum major" quote be removed. They thought it made King sound arrogant. But there was one problem. The quote was carved into the granite. In 2012, the U.S. Secretary of the Interior, who is in charge of national parks, monuments, and other public land, ordered the quote's removal. Lei returned in 2013 to replace the quote with carved grooves himself. It cost $800,000 to make the change.

National Mall Monuments

As the National Mall's first monument to honor an African American, the Martin Luther King, Jr. Memorial is a must-see on any trip to Washington D.C. If you ever get to visit, make sure to check out some of the other nearby memorials to people and events that have left a mark on U.S. history.

Lincoln Memorial

Completed: 1922

Honors: President Abraham Lincoln, who worked to keep the country together during the Civil War (1861–1865)

Fact: This monument is shown on the back of the penny and the $5 bill.

World War II Memorial

Completed: 2004

Honors: The millions of Americans who served during World War II

Fact: One wall of the memorial has 4,048 stars fastened onto it. Each star represents 100 of the more than 400,000 Americans who died in the war.

Korean War Veterans Memorial

Completed: 1995

Honors: Americans who fought for a democratic government in Korea between 1950 and 1953

Fact: The artist who sculpted the 19 statues of soldiers, sailors, and airmen for the memorial fought in World War II.

Washington Monument

Completed: 1884

Honors: The United States' first president, George Washington

Fact: Builders were forced to halt the construction of this monument for several years because of the Civil War (1861–1865).

Vietnam Veterans Memorial

Completed: 1982

Honors: The Americans who died or went missing in the Vietnam War (1954–1975)

Fact: While most war memorials list names in order of rank, the more than 58,000 names on this memorial's giant wall are in order of death or disappearance.

OUT OF THE MOUNTAIN OF DESPAIR,
A STONE OF HOPE

A Stone of Hope

A sentence from Dr. King's "I Have a Dream" speech inspired the memorial's design: "With this faith, we will be able to hew [carve] out of the mountain of despair a stone of hope." The memorial has a central path that leads between two granite boulders. Separated by a walkway, those stones symbolize a path through the "mountain of despair."

The central statue includes the words that inspired the memorial's design.

Hope from Despair

King's figure emerges from the "Stone of Hope" and appears to be gazing across the Tidal Basin. The park was designed to make it look as if the Stone of Hope had moved forward, out of the gap in the two boulders that are the "Mountain of Despair."

The 30-foot (9 m) sculpture of King is taller than the statues of Lincoln and Jefferson at nearby memorials.

Stone of Hope

Visitors walk through the monument.

Mountain of Despair

President Barack Obama and his family walk along the memorial's wall with King's family.

A 450-foot (137 m) crescent-shaped wall curves behind the boulders. The wall's design was inspired by a sermon King delivered in 1965. He said, "We shall overcome because the arc of the moral universe is long but it bends towards justice." The curving wall represents the arc of the moral universe King describes.

Fourteen Quotes

The 14 quotes carved into the wall come from speeches and sermons King delivered from 1955 until his death in 1968. A Council of Historians chose each of the quotes. Members included poet Maya Angelou and historian Henry Louis Gates Jr. The quotes discuss themes such as justice, democracy, hope, and love. They paint a picture of the ways King fought for equality, and how he encouraged others to fight alongside him.

Timeline of the Memorial's Creation

1968

Dr. King is assassinated.

1983

The Alpha Phi Alpha fraternity begins planning a memorial.

1996

U.S. Congress decides that public land can be used for the memorial.

The Dedication

The memorial was dedicated, or opened to the public, on August 25, 2011. The dedication was planned as a weekend celebration. But a dangerous hurricane swept through the area during the weekend and speeches were postponed. Even so, the Alpha Phi Alpha fraternity went forward with a private celebration that attracted 5,000 people. The rescheduled public celebration was held on October 16, with a speech from President Barack Obama. Ten thousand people attended.

2007
Lei Yixin is selected to carve the monument.

2011
The Martin Luther King, Jr. Memorial opens to the public.

2000
Planners choose a memorial design by ROMA Design Group.

2010
A cargo ship with the memorial's granite blocks arrives in Baltimore, Maryland.

Cherry blossoms bloom each spring, marking the season during which Martin Luther King Jr. died.

The Park Today

More than 3 million people visit the Martin Luther King, Jr. Memorial every year. Open 24 hours every day, it is free to the public. The land around the memorial is filled with cherry trees, crape myrtles, winter jasmine, and other plants. The spring is especially beautiful when the cherry trees bloom.

National Mall and Memorial Parks is a special department within the National Park Service. It is responsible for all of Washington, D.C.'s national memorials, and it takes care of the King memorial.

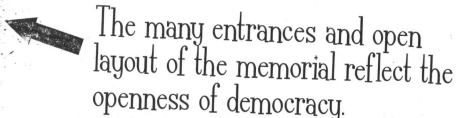
The many entrances and open layout of the memorial reflect the openness of democracy.

Don't forget to ask for a map at a ranger station or the White House Visitor Center. The King memorial is one of several included on a special map with activities.

Experiencing the Memorial

If you visit, remember to find a park ranger. The rangers work at the memorial from 9:30 a.m. until 10 p.m. every day. They offer guided tours on bike and on foot throughout the National Mall. As you look around at the King memorial, remember all the work that was done not only by the monument's creators, but also by the man the memorial honors. King and his monument will inspire hope in millions for many years to come. ★

Tidal Basin Reservoir

Built in the 1800s, the Tidal Basin **reservoir** is 107 acres (43 hectares) in size and 10 feet (3 m) deep. About 250 million gallons (946 million liters) of water flow between it and the Potomac River at high tide. Visitors wanting to view the King memorial from the water can rent swan boats and paddleboats. A walking trail winds around the reservoir. It's lined with 3,000 cherry trees, a gift from Japan.

The Washington Monument is visible to the northeast of the Tidal Basin.

National Mall Map Mystery

This building's rotunda—a round, domed room—holds a bust of Martin Luther King Jr. and many other important people. National laws are written and passed here. Follow the directions below to find this building. What is its name?

The White House

National Museum of African American History And Culture

Constitution Ave NW

Lincoln Memorial

Vietnam Veterans Memorial

Washington Monument

Reflecting Pool

Korean War Veterans Memorial

World War II Memorial

Independence Ave SW

Kutz Bridge

Martin Luther King, Jr. Memorial

Tidal Basin

Potomac River

Thomas Jefferson Memorial

Directions

1. Start at the Martin Luther King, Jr. Memorial.

2. Walk east across the Tidal Basin on the Kutz Bridge, then north toward a tall monument that honors our first president.

3. Take the DC Circulator bus east along Jefferson Drive, past Smithsonian Castle and several other museums.

4. Get off at the corner just east of a museum devoted to the continent's first people. Almost there!

5. Continue walking east, around a large reflecting pool, to an important building where Congress meets. Inside, you'll find King's bust. Where are you?

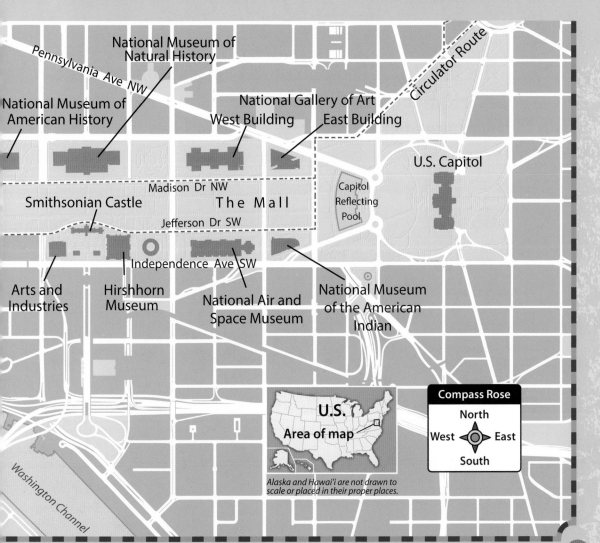

Be a Memorial Explorer!

The District of Columbia offers places to find African American memorials and historic sites. Here are a few. If you are visiting the city, see if you can find them all.

Bust of Sojourner Truth

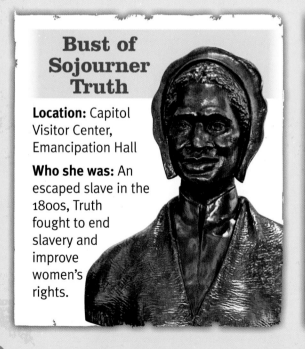

Location: Capitol Visitor Center, Emancipation Hall

Who she was: An escaped slave in the 1800s, Truth fought to end slavery and improve women's rights.

Rosa Parks Statue

Location: U.S. Capitol, Nationa[l] Statuary Hall

Who she was: Parks fought for civil rights alongside Marti[n] Luther King Jr. Her arrest on an Alabama bus in 1955 sparked a major bus boycott.

Frederick Douglass National Historic Site

Location: 1411 W Street SE

Who he was: Douglass escaped slavery in 1838 to become an outspoken writer, speaker, and politician.

Mary McLeod Bethune Memorial and the Council House National Historic Site

Locations: Lincoln Park and 1318 Vermont Ave NW

Who she was: Bethune worked to improve the lives of African Americans, particularly in education, throughout the first half of the 20th century.

"Spirit of Freedom"

Location: 10th and U Streets NW

What it is: This memorial honors the African Americans who fought during the Civil War (1861–1865).

A. Philip Randolph Monument

Location: 50 Massachusetts Ave NE, Union Station

Who he was: Randolph fought for the rights of African American workers in the 20th century.

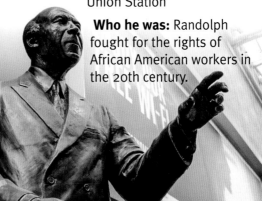

True Statistics

Number of granite blocks used to build the memorial: 159

Total weight of granite stones used: 1,764 tons

Distance from Washington, D.C., to Lei Yixin's studio in China: 11,000 mi. (17,703 km)

Length of the sculpture's voyage from China to Baltimore, Maryland: 47 days

Exact height of King's statue: 30 ft. 8 in. (9.3 m)

Weight of granite stone used to carve Dr. King's head: 46 tons

Size of land used for the memorial: 4 acres (1.6 ha)

Number of countries that submitted designs for the memorial: 52

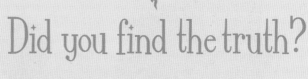

Did you find the truth?

(T) The Martin Luther King, Jr. Memorial was made in China.

(F) The monument was approved and built just 10 years after King's death.

Resources

Books

Dorling Kindersley staff. *Eyewitness Travel 2017: Washington, DC*. New York: DK Publishing, 2016.

Kennedy, Barbara Noe. *Walking Washington, D.C.: The Best of the City*. Washington, DC: National Geographic, 2017.

Mattern, Joanne. *Martin Luther King, Jr. National Memorial: A Stone of Hope*. South Egremont, MA: Red Chair Press, 2018.

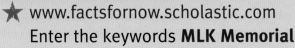

Visit this Scholastic website for more information on Martin Luther King, Jr. Memorial:

★ www.factsfornow.scholastic.com
Enter the keywords **MLK Memorial**

Important Words

activist (AK-tih-vist) a person who takes strong actions in support of or against one side of an issue

boycott (BOI-kaht) a refusal to buy something or do business with someone as a punishment or protest

civil rights (SIV-uhl RITES) the individual rights that all members of a democratic society have to freedom and equal treatment under the law

discrimination (dis-krim-uh-NAY-shuhn) the unfair treatment of someone

fraternity (fruh-TUR-nuh-tee) a men's student organization formed mainly for social purposes and having a name with Greek letters

models (MAH-duhlz) things that someone builds as an example of something larger, to see how it will work or look

monument (MAHN-yuh-muhnt) a statue, building, or other structure that reminds people of an event or a person

reservoir (REZ-ur-vwahr) a natural or human-made lake in which water is collected and stored for use

resolution (rez-uh-LOO-shuhn) a formal vote or decision

segregation (seg-rih-GAY-shuhn) the act or practice of keeping people or groups apart based on race, gender, religion, or other factors

Index

Page numbers in **bold** indicate illustrations.

About the Author

Christine Taylor-Butler has written more than 80 books for children including the True Book series on American Government, The Human Body, and Science Experiments. She is also the author of the middle grade science-fiction fantasy series The Lost Tribes. A graduate of MIT, Christine holds degrees in both civil engineering and art and design. She currently lives in Kansas City, Missouri.